Welcome to the first short collection of poetry from *Ha

Before we go anywhere… I want to say a big, heart-felt **Th**

Thank you for being one of the special souls to which this book was attracted to.

Thank you for supporting art and poetry. It's because of you that this
book was even created in the first place… In one sense…

You are the very reason that this book came to be.

As well as writing poetry, I am passionate about sharing the power of the pen and paper as
a tool for self-therapy, emotional release and for manifesting the future of your dreams.

I'm on the path of living a life on my own terms and creating the life of my dreams –
and I'm determined to take as many people as possible on that path with me…

For we all deserve to live the life of our grandest desires.

Now, I use the skills I have learnt in my own life to help others make
great transformations and breakthroughs in their lives.

As well as offering one-on-one life coaching and hypnotherapy, I also devise life-changing,
immersive retreats in magical places. In this way – I have created the opportunity for us to
work together on a much deeper level to make profound shifts and personal evolution.

Full details of everything I do, along with more poetry, videos of some of my performances,
all my contact details and more can be found on my website – http://www.hartfloe.com

My mission on Earth is to serve Humanity to the highest

degree – using my own special and unique talents to inspire, empower and elevate those souls who I am lucky enough to cross paths with.

The deep love in my heart goes into everything I do – from the writing of these words to the creation and facilitation of my retreats and everything in between…

I hope and trust that you will feel that love connecting with your heart through the vibration of my intention.

If you do… then do what you can to spread that love on – *to 'pay it forward'* – and to be another agent for light and love in this world… working together to create a brighter tomorrow for those that will follow.

From my heart straight to yours.
Hart Floe Poet

♥

Life's Too Short

A collection of short poems written to remind you to fly as free as the butterflies, the birds and the bees… and truly create any life that you please.

By Hart Floe Poet

They always say that *"Life's Too Short."* …

And in many ways I agree.

Life is too short to *hold back.*
Life is too short to *not give your gifts.*
To be *scared…*
To play small…
To live under your greatness.

Life is too short to *waste time doubting yourself* and your abilities.

It's too short to spend time *regretting the past* or *worrying about the future…*

This moment *is all we really have.*

The eternal moment of **Now.**

Eternal…

That doesn't sound *too short* now does it??!

And you're right… *it's not…*

Life will go on forever.

It is *infinite* and *never-ending.*

And yet… *still it is too short.*

It's too short to *waste time trying to be **something you're not**...*
Or *trying to reject **who you are.***
It's too short to go round *blaming* and *complaining* and ***giving your power away** to others.*
It's too short to not ***make your dreams into your reality...***

*That would just be **insanity.***

So seize the moment... This is **YOUR** time... so *take it* and
use it in the *most magical way* that you can...

Create a life of *happiness, joy, bliss* and *inspiration.*
Be a light in the dark. Become the superstar that you are destined to be.

After all... that's what you came here for, right??! ...
To shine bright?
Alright – So go ahead and let that fire inside you **IGNITE** –
*For Life Is Too Short to not **take flight.***

When You *Give…*
You **Grow**

It's *Your Life*
∞
Live
∞
In The Flow

To Watch a Butterfly Spread Her Wings,
Is such a beautiful thing…

It's not just the feeling of pleasure it brings,
But the sound of its freedom that rings…

It will make your soul sing.

From this moment onward,
I'll no longer hold back…
I won't let my fear -
Knock me off track.

So *that's why* I'm here…
Sharing this truth.
I hope I'll inspire you,
To ***be true to you*** too.

A canopy of *such complete complexion* -
You can't help but *fall into introspection*.

On deeper reflection,
It's easy to see…

**We Need the Trees,
So We Can Breathe.**

When you want to quit and throw in the towel...

Think of the **'Why'**...

Then you'll figure out *'How'*.

Although we are many…

We are only 'One'.

Just like this rainbow that danced around the sun.

Everything goes in circles…
The cycles repeat forever.

The moon comes up as the sun goes down,
As we ride through this circus together.

Slow and steady wins the race…

Rushing through you miss the view.

Soon ending up in the wrong place,

Forgetting –

What was true for you??

A safe distance from the city –
From the busy-nitty-gritty.

Breathing healing mountain air,
With landscapes oh-so-pretty.

Though one day I'm sure I must return...
What a pity.

Reach up,
Reach out,
and touch the sky…

You never needed wings in order to fly.

Such a *beautifully complex* and *perfect* design,
Reflecting the *infinite possibilities* of the divine.

To bloom into something so glorious takes time -

Patience.

Searching for something outside
that *can only be found within...*

Looking for somewhere to hide,

From the shadow that's cast by our sin.
§∞§∞§∞§∞§∞§

On A Side Note –
I don't believe in sin. There is no inherent 'right' or 'wrong'...
*They are **labels** that we choose to place on things, which ultimately dictates our fate.*
*What we **DECIDE** is 'right' or 'wrong' forms the answer to the question –*
***'Who Am I?'** – Who do I define myself to be?*

*There are **no mistakes**, only **learning opportunities.***
*There are **no failures**, only **feedback.***
*True and lasting **happiness exists within** and cannot be provided by external circumstances.*

§∞§∞§∞§∞§∞§

Focusing on gratitude removes the possibility of misery.

The Sea…

So vast.

It wears no masks yet masks so much of the unknown beneath its surface –
We are blind.

∞

It reminds me *there's still so much more* for me to find –
Beneath the surface of my mind.

**Just need to keep on
diving
d
e
e
p
e
r
…**

Liquid gold to charred coal,
Like an oil painting that ignites the soul.

It looks *so young* but is *infinitely old,*
and holds within it -
Every tale ever told.

Soothing serenity of the splashing streams.

Lulling lullabies lead to lucid dreams……
……..
…
..
.
There's so much more to life than it seems.

Looking to the sky…
In a state of contemplation.

Gratitude and love…
Rest in deep appreciation.

Picture perfect sunsets,
Bring serenity and bliss.

Such awe-inspiring beauty,
Is **impossible** *to miss.*

You should *never judge a book by its cover*.
In fact, you should never really judge it by the content within -
It's *between the lines*,
In the *subconscious mind*,
Where the truth really begins.

Because -
You don't know when the words were written…
Or where they were conceived,
Or what lead to their creation,
What inspiration they received.
Or what past events had to occur,
Or what pain, hurt or suffering,
Was previously incurred,
That resulted in those words.

So don't judge -
Even if you've read the book,
Maybe several times,
To understand it fully -
You will need another look.
Even then there might be more,
That rests below - *just out of sight.*
But you can help them see the truth,
By giving them your light.

So shine your light on every page,
Release your love through every age,
Pick the lock on every cage,
And give your gifts from every stage.

Remember to love the trees...

They're the reason we can breathe.

∞ The river *only knows* ∞
∞ **How** ∞ **to** ∞ **be** ∞ **in** ∞ **flow** ∞

No matter the obstacles –
It never slows.

The construction of a deep connection *from one soul to another* -
Is a long-term labour of love and devotion.
=
The destruction of that bridge is a path that's paved with *confusion and difficult emotion.*
=
But a well-made bridge will **never crumble…**
and can cross the widest ocean.
=
=
Bridges.

Everything's impermanent - *Nothing lasts forever.*

Even if you want to - *You can't always be together.*

Acceptance makes things better.

Branches reach out *to touch the light,*
Branches breathe out - *day and night.*
Branches branch out - in *every direction,*

Y

All branches join at the same intersection.

Everything is **linked∞&∞connected**…
Interrelated in some way.
Science has proven that now so there's no need for another debate on that today.
But consciousness…
How can we define that better?
Well…
Consciousness is the invisible energy that *strings it all together.*

From the *human form* to the *raging storm*…
From the *skies above* to the *feeling of love* -

Consciousness is the constant that has been here forever.

I don't *have a consciousness*…
I AM consciousness.
I'm *not aware* that I am alive…
I AM *that awareness*…
And so are you too.

When you go back far enough,
Everything originates from the same source of energy –
We know this much is true…

So the consciousness that runs through me is the same that runs through you.

I'm your *ancient cosmic brother,*
and you're my sister too…
Even if we never knew.

But now we do.

So *that's* consciousness…
From the *worm in the ground,*
To *every vibration of sound.*
Every *beam of light…*
To every *sparkle in the night,*
And every *twinkle in every eye.*

That's consciousness…
It's so much more than science has defined.

Perfectly still reflections lead to deepened introspection.

I sit alone,
my hand in my own,
and water all the seeds I've sewn.

When the chaos of storm clouds gather around,

To dismay and distress you find yourself bound...

Looking within is where peace can be found.

They say that history repeats itself -

Like the cyclic dancing of the waves and the pulling of the tides.

You end up in the same place,
with a different person,
a different face...

Still telling yourself lies.

You just need some time to look inside.

Dreamy scenes of beauty, serenity and bliss…
As the sun was dripping down it slipped its fire on his wrist.

In that fleeting moment…
He was truly sun-kissed.

There's this feeling inside that I just cannot hide...

I'm holding on tight and prepared for the ride.

Sharp shards of seductive rays that dance across the shimmering lake.

As they penetrate my soul they remind me that *my dreams are always mine to make...*

And too...

That they are mine to break.

When life's a struggle and becomes a blur…
Just focus your energy on *what you'd prefer.*

What ideally do you want to occur?

Get crystal clear on a focused vision..

Then *break off from the herd,*
and **never be deterred**,
from letting your wishes be heard.

Be **loud** and **clear**,
Move past your fear,
and then give thanks…

For Just Being Here.

A wickedly-warped-wooden-wormhole of wonder...

Sometimes the surreal beauty of mother nature can break the spell you're under...

Nature wakes you from your slumber.

The trees are truly what we need.

Without these lungs - ours cannot breathe.

It's a *simple truth* that's easy to see -

Just like ours, when you cut them,
They bleed.
=
=
= __.*Stop.Cutting.Please.*__ =

When galaxies are born and new stars are taking form…
Find the courage to face the storm.

Because you're destined for something more.

When you find yourself enticed into conflict,
Crashing head-to-head –

Remember the truth that a war won't solve things…

Instead of hatred,
Choose love instead.

Ignore all the haters,
Just leave them for now.
'Cause when you reach the top…
You can show them all how.

But if you ***never stop,***
*You'll just **keep on going.***
The seeds that you sew *will just **keep on growing,***
And the garden you tender that was once full of weeds,
Will suddenly sprout all the roots, shoots and leaves,
That will flower and blossom if you just…

Believe.

As the sun slips into a pocket in the sky…

So Sublime.
So Divine.

It brings tears to the eye.

I forgot I was there,
Whilst I was lost in you.
I forgot about me,
Mesmerised by the view.

.

.

.

.

Don't lose 'you' when 'one' becomes 'two.'

Those autumn leaves that tumble down and paint the ground with golden brown.

Walking through, dazed and dreamy, crunchy footsteps - hypnotic sound.

Summer's over...
Winter-bound.

You paint a picture *perfect future,* then tell the world of your creation.
Tell it with *power,* with *passion* and *conviction.*
The future you experience is born from your predictions…

If you predict you'll fail,
That's probably what you'll do.
If you predict that you'll succeed,
You'll probably get that too…

So Try Predicting Something New.

The canopy of leaves permitting only certain rays.

The magic of the trees can leave me sitting in a haze.

Whenever they are close,
I find I'm dreaming in the day.

Even when you can barely see through,
Know that you have endless power in you.

You may not believe it but *trust me...*

It's true.

The mightiest solar giant,
Upon which our whole life is reliant.

=

You were my very own raging inferno,
But there was something I had to learn though…

=

I had to learn how to let you go…

=

And still shine on with my own special glow.

Surrender to the wind's caress.
Let it gently clear your weighted chest.

Don't be afraid to **ask**…

The universe *WANTS* to help you…

If you'll just give it half a chance.

On those days where the sun would melt into the sea...
I knew I was where I was meant to be.

Holding my own hand as I nurtured the seed,
That will one day grow into a powerful tree.

We are **Giants** by nature.
Our *craving for creation* is **Ginormous.**
Our *capacity for compassion* is **Gargantuan.**
Our *lust for love* is **Limitless.**
Our *potential for progression* is **Infinite.**

=

=

=

We are giants... But we spend our lives crouching.

=

Stand tall…
And you may have it all.

That raging inferno –
The fire that burns infinitely in our skies as the day turns to night.

Like the smouldering core of the Earth –
Let that fire fuel the birth of a new you,
With every passing moment.

Because we can always burn brighter.

Forks in your path.
Crossroads ahead…

Y

Follow your heart instead of your head.

You can change the past by reflecting back.

You will struggle in the present by *rejecting facts.*

Solid stone stories *beginning to crack.*

The ones for so long you've loved to re-enact.
.
.

- Fables

That golden light that shines through the trees…

It shines through you as it shines through me.

Peering through the curtain of your *wildest dreams and desires.*

Dive through and I'm certain that *those dreams will blast you higher.*

You were born to be a high flyer -
Just Trust.

There's a *magic in the mountains* that will *make the mayhem mellow out...*

The calmness and serenity will sooth your mind and soul no doubt.

I want to make you feel the beauty that you fail to see.

I want to help you spread your wings so that you can fly free.

I want to bring you just that little bit closer to me -

Destiny.

Epic glare as the sun flares…
I stand and stare –
Giving thanks that it's there.

Its invigorating rays that brighten our days,
I'm sat there amazed that it's so far away.

The light of its love knows no other way.
=
=
- Distance.

So don't delay....

Go and create your wildest dreams today!
Make a Movement. Shake Things Up…
For life truly is too short to let them slip away.

Connect with me and let's bring more light and love
into this world together at www.hartfloe.com

With Love Always…
In All Ways.
Hart Floe Poet.

Lightning Source UK Ltd.
Milton Keynes UK
UKHW051619020919
348934UK00003B/25/P

AuthorHouse™ UK
1663 Liberty Drive
Bloomington, IN 47403 USA
www.authorhouse.co.uk
Phone: 0800 047 8203 (Domestic TFN)
+44 1908 723714 (International)

Published by AuthorHouse 06/14/2019

ISBN: 978-1-7283-8948-6 (sc)
ISBN: 978-1-7283-8947-9 (e)

Library of Congress Control Number: 2019907519

Print information available on the last page.

Any people depicted in stock imagery provided by Getty Images are models,
and such images are being used for illustrative purposes only.
Certain stock imagery © Getty Images.

This book is printed on acid-free paper.

authorHOUSE®

Life's Too Short

A collection of short poems written to remind you to fly as free as the butterflies,
the birds and the bees… and truly create any life that you please.

H A R T   F L O E   P O E T